PIANO • VOCAL • GUITAR

2012 GREATEST Pop & Rock Hits

MW01102458

THE BIGGEST HITS ★ DELUXE ANNUAL EDITION

THE GREATEST ARTISTS

CONTENTS

Song	Artist	Page
Best Thing I Never Had	Beyoncé	2
The Big Bang Theory (Main Title Theme)	Barenaked Ladies	10
Body and Soul	Tony Bennett and Amy Winehouse	16
Cough Syrup	Young the Giant	21
Domino	Jessie J.	30
Greatest Love of All	Whitney Houston	42
Here's to Us	Halestorm, *Glee* Cast	37
House	Ben Folds Five	46
Human Nature	Michael Jackson, *Glee* Cast	53
If I Die Young	The Band Perry	60
It Will Rain	Bruno Mars	68
Jar of Hearts	Christina Perri	82
Just a Kiss	Lady Antebellum	76
Keep Your Head Up	Andy Grammer	89
Kiss Me Slowly	Parachute	98
The Lady Is a Tramp	Tony Bennett and Lady Gaga	105
Last Friday Night (T.G.I.F.)	Katy Perry	114
Let Me Be Your Star	*Smash* Cast	121
Love You Like a Love Song	Selena Gomez & The Scene	130
Monster	Paramore	136
Mr. Know It All	Kelly Clarkson	142
Not Over You	Gavin DeGraw	149
One Moment in Time	Whitney Houston	158
The One That Got Away	Katy Perry	163
Price Tag	Jessie J featuring B.o.B	170
Red Solo Cup	Toby Keith	200
Smooth Criminal	Michael Jackson, *Glee* Cast	176
Soldier	Gavin DeGraw	188
Somebody That I Used to Know	Gotye featuring Kimbra	194
We Are Young	fun	207
When We Stand Together	Nickelback	220
Who Says	Selena Gomez & The Scene	214

Produced by
Alfred Music Publishing Co., Inc.
P.O. Box 10003
Van Nuys, CA 91410-0003
alfred.com

Printed in USA.

ISBN-10: 0-7390-8919-6
ISBN-13: 978-0-7390-8919-4

Alfred Cares. Contents printed on 100% recycled paper.

BEST THING I NEVER HAD

Words and Music by
SHEA TAYLOR, ANTONIO DIXON,
KENNETH "BABYFACE" EDMONDS,
LARRY GRIFFIN, JR., BEYONCÉ KNOWLES,
CALED McCAMPBELL and PATRICK "J. QUE" SMITH

Moderately ♩ = 100

*Original recording up 1/2 step in F♯.

Best Thing I Never Had - 8 - 1

Best Thing I Never Had - 8 - 2

THE BIG BANG THEORY
Main Title Theme (Album Length Version)

Words and Music by
ED ROBERTSON and
STEVEN PAGE

The Big Bang Theory - 6 - 1

Verse 3:

3. Aus - tra - lo - pith - e - cus would real - ly have been sick of us, de - bat - ing how we're here. They're catch - ing

15

BODY AND SOUL

Words by
EDWARD HEYMAN, ROBERT SOUR
and FRANK EYTON

Music by
JOHN GREEN

18

Body and Soul - 5 - 3

COUGH SYRUP

Words and Music by
SAMEER GADHIA, ERIC CANNATA,
JACOB TILLEY, FRANCOIS COMTOIS
and EHSON HASHEMIAN

Medium rock ♩ = 132

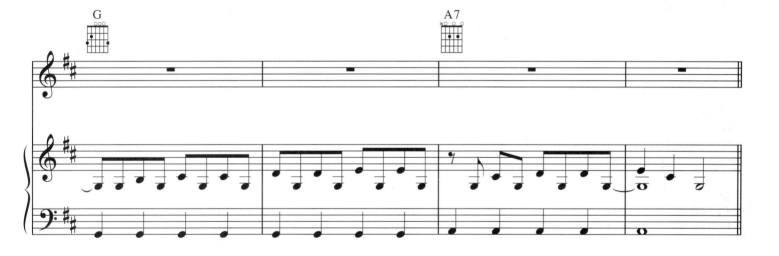

Verse:

1. Life's too short to ev-en care at all,___ oh, whoa._____
2. Life's too short to ev-en care at all,___ oh, whoa._____

Cough Syrup - 9 - 1

22

Cough Syrup - 9 - 2

come down.

now. And so I run now to the things they say could re - store _ me,

DOMINO

Words and Music by
KELLY, LUKASZ GOTTWALD,
MAX MARTIN, HENRY WALTER
and JESSICA CORNISH

Moderate dance rock ♩ = 120

Domino - 7 - 1

34

Domino - 7 - 6

HERE'S TO US

Words and Music by
LIZZY HALE, TOBY GAD
and DANIELLE BRISEBOIS

Moderate rock ♩ = 80

Verse 1 (sing 1st time only):

1. We could just___ go home___ right now,___ or may-be we___ could stick a-round___ for

Verse 2 (sing 2nd time only):

stuck it out___ this far___ to-geth-er, put our dreams___ through the shred-der. Let's

just one___ more drink, oh yeah.___

toast, 'cause things got bet-ter. And ev-

GREATEST LOVE OF ALL

Words by
LINDA CREED

Music by
MICHAEL MASSER

1.3. I be-lieve the chil-dren are our fu-ture; teach them well and let them lead the way.
be. 2. Ev-'ry-bod-y's search-ing for a he-ro; peo-ple need some-one to look up to.

Show them all the beau-ty they pos-sess in-side. Give them a
I nev-er found an-y - one who ful-filled my needs. A lone-ly

Greatest Love of All - 4 - 1

HOUSE

Words and Music by
BEN FOLDS

House - 7 - 1

50 *Chorus:*

And I could go___ there, but I'm not go - ing,

pulse is slow - ing, no, I'm not ner-vous an - y-more.

I've seen the night - mares, and seen some coun - sellors,

but I'm not go - ing back up in that house_ a -

Chorus:

HUMAN NATURE

Words and Music by
JEFF PORCARO and JOHN BETTIS

Human Nature - 7 - 1

56

Repeat and fade

IF I DIE YOUNG

Words and Music by
KIMBERLY PERRY

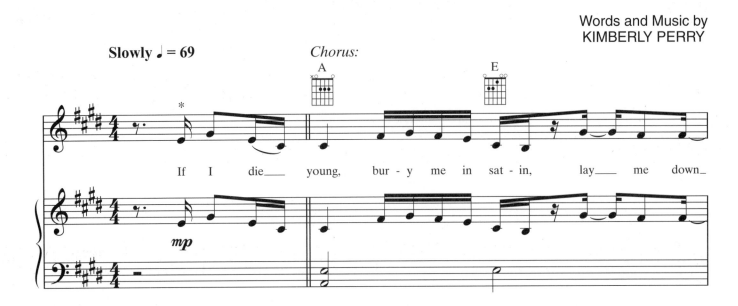

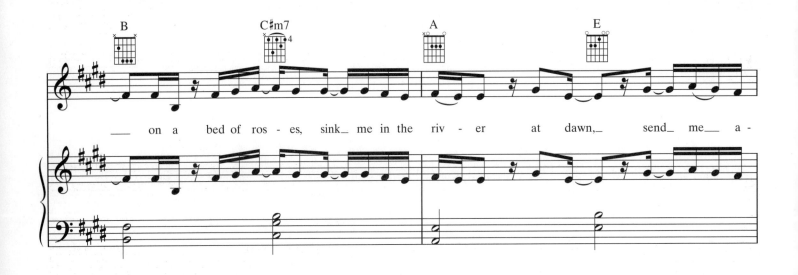

*All vocals written at pitch.

If I Die Young - 8 - 1

62

Chorus:

If I die___ young, bur-y me in sat-in, lay___ me down___ on a bed of ros-es, sink___ me in the riv-er at dawn,___ send___ me___ a-way___ with the words of a love song. The sharp___ knife of a short___ life.___ Well, I've_____ had just e-nough

64

Well, I've had just e-nough time.

So put on your best boys and I'll wear my pearls.

Bridge:

mp   *rit.*

IT WILL RAIN

Words and Music by
BRUNO MARS, PHILIP LAWRENCE
and ARI LEVINE

It Will Rain - 8 - 2

70

73

It Will Rain - 8 - 6

Chorus:

JUST A KISS

Words and Music by
CHARLES KELLEY, DAVE HAYWOOD,
HILLARY SCOTT and DALLAS DAVIDSON

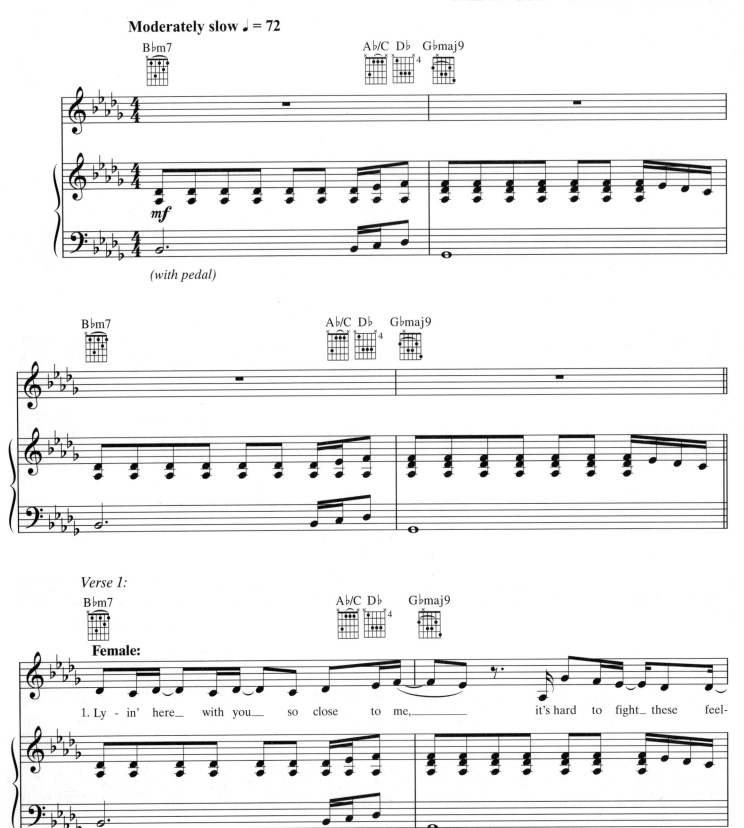

Just a Kiss - 6 - 1

ings when it feels_ so hard to breathe.____ I'm caught up in___ this mo-

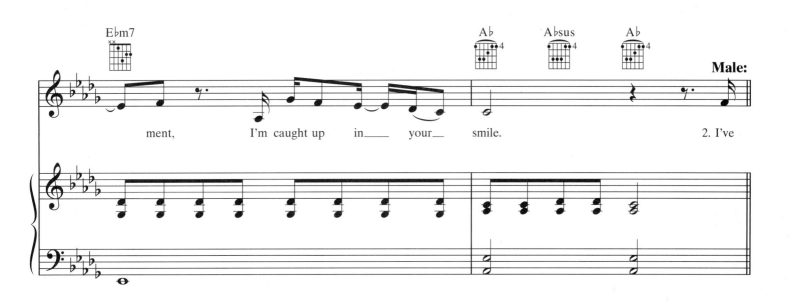

ment, I'm caught up in____ your_ smile. 2. I've

Verse 2 (sing 1st time only):

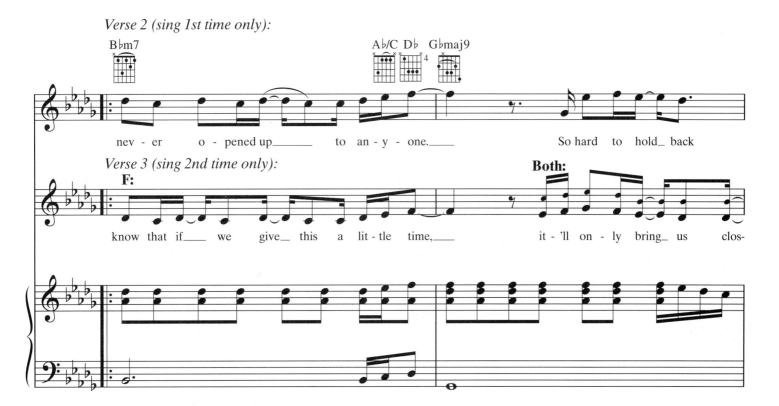

nev - er o - pened up_____ to an - y - one.____ So hard to hold_ back

Verse 3 (sing 2nd time only):

F:

know that if___ we give_ this a lit - tle time,___ it - 'll on - ly bring_ us clos-

Coda

JAR OF HEARTS

Words and Music by
DREW LAWRENCE, CHRISTINA PERRI
and BARRETT YERETSIAN

88

from the ice in - side__ your soul. Don't come back for

me. Don't come back at all.

Who do you think you__ are? Who do you think you__

____ are? Who do you think you are?

rall.

KEEP YOUR HEAD UP

Words and Music by
ANDY GRAMMER

92

Verse 2:

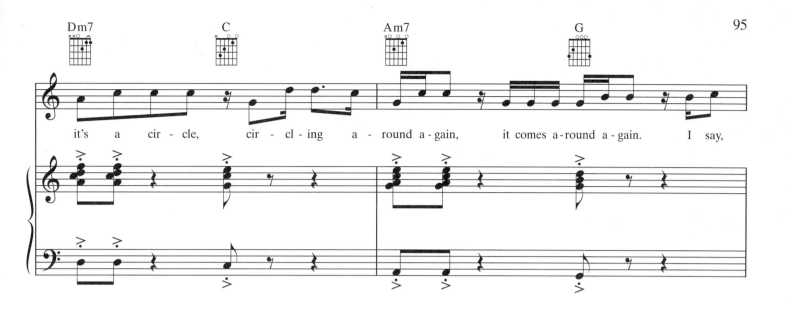

it's a cir - cle, cir - cl - ing a - round a - gain, it comes a - round a - gain. I say,

on - ly rain - bows af - ter rain. The sun will al - ways come a - gain. And

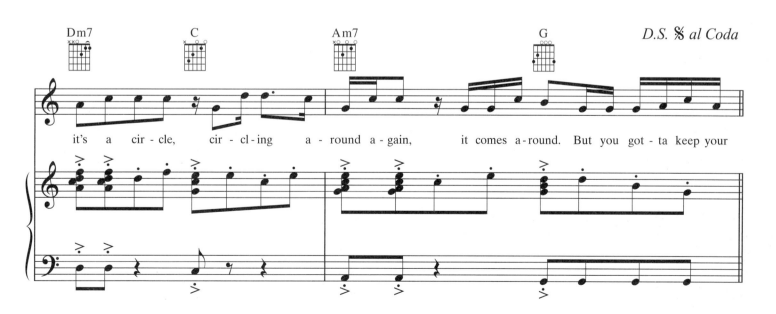

it's a cir - cle, cir - cl - ing a - round a - gain, it comes a - round. But you got - ta keep your

D.S. % al Coda

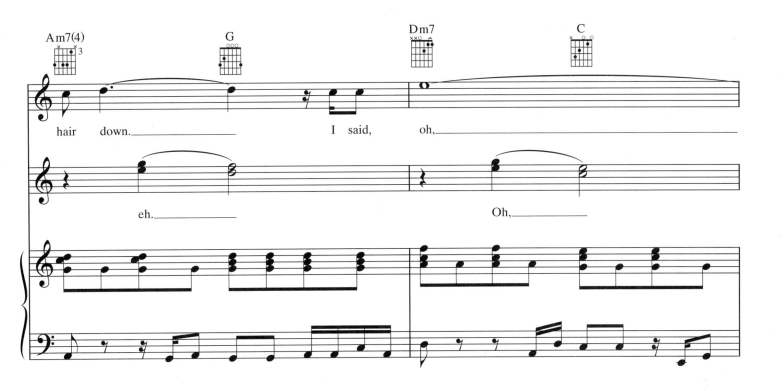

KISS ME SLOWLY

102

kiss me slow - ly.

Don't run__ a - way.__

And it's hard__ to love__ a - gain,__

THE LADY IS A TRAMP

Words by
LORENZ HART

Music by
RICHARD RODGERS

The Lady Is a Tramp - 9 - 7

LAST FRIDAY NIGHT

(T.G.I.F.)

Words and Music by
KATY PERRY, LUKASZ GOTTWALD,
MAX MARTIN, BENJAMIN LEVIN
and BONNIE MCKEE

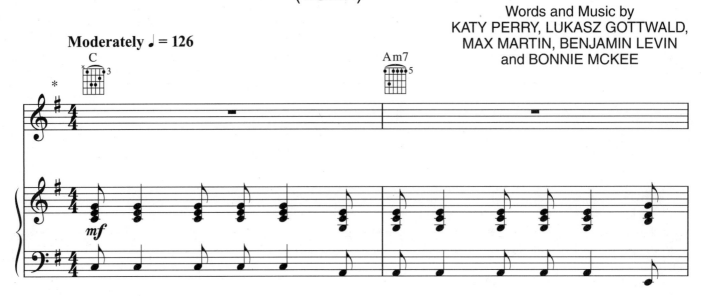

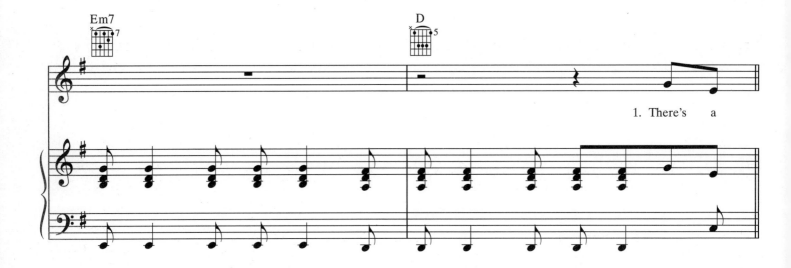

1. There's a

Verse:

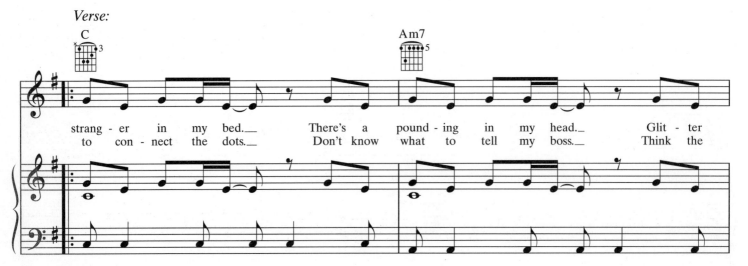

strang-er in my bed.__ There's a pound-ing in my head.__ Glit-ter
to con-nect the dots.__ Don't know what to tell my boss.__ Think the

*Recorded in F♯ major.

Last Friday Night - 7 - 1

116

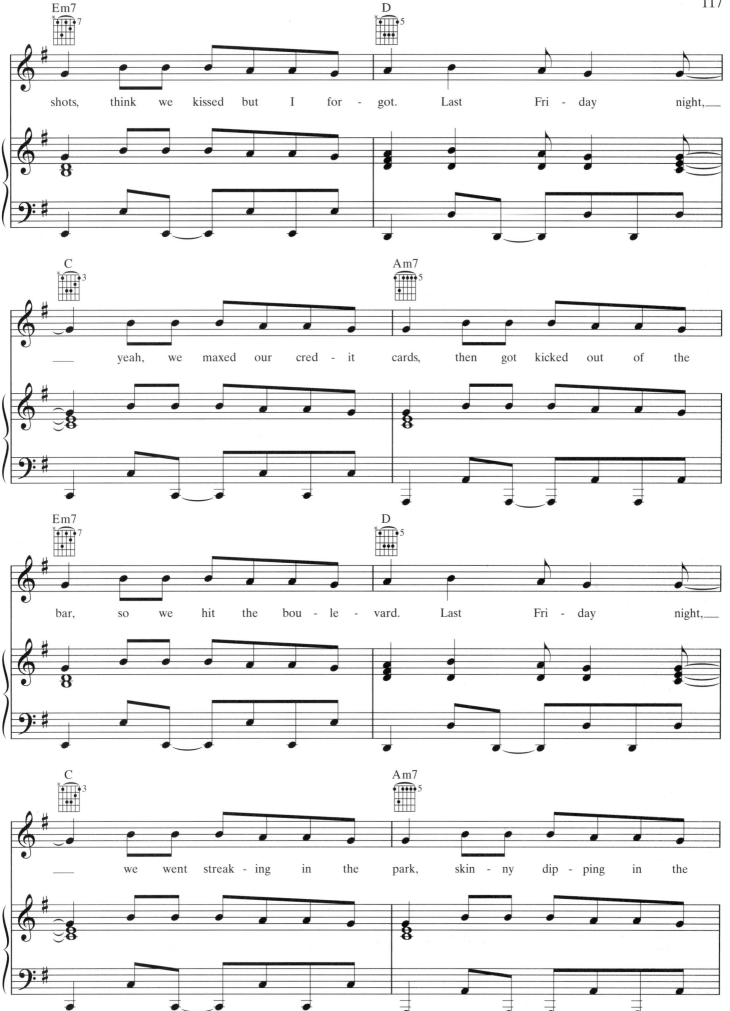

118

120

LET ME BE YOUR STAR

Lyrics by
SCOTT WITTMAN and MARC SHAIMAN

Music by
MARC SHAIMAN

Moderately bright (♩ = 143)

Intro:

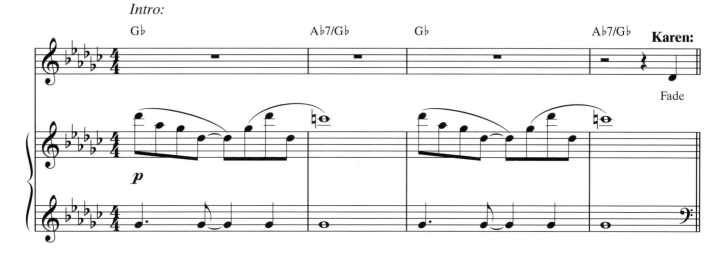

Verse 1:

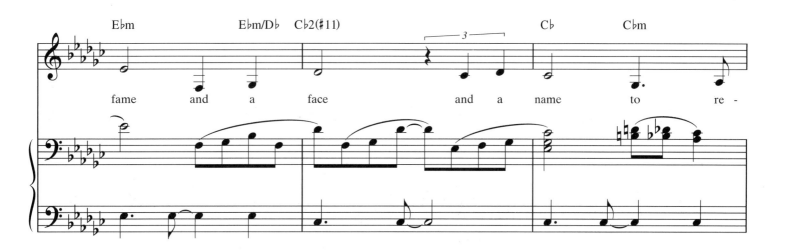

Let Me Be Your Star - 9 - 1

122

123

Let Me Be Your Star - 9 - 3

124

LOVE YOU LIKE A LOVE SONG

Words and Music by
ANTONINA ARMATO, ADAM SCHMALHOLZ
and TIM JAMES

133

MONSTER

Words and Music by
HAYLEY WILLIAMS and TAYLOR YORK

gone,___ the world is ours.

Bridge:

Well, you found the strength_ in so - lu - tions,

MR. KNOW IT ALL

Words and Music by
BRETT JAMES, ESTER DEAN,
BRIAN KENNEDY and DANTE JONES

Verse 1:

1. Mis - ter know_ it all, well, you, you think you know_ it all, but you don't know a thing_ at all. Ain't it, ain't it some - thing, y'all, when some - bod - y tells you some-thin' 'bout you, think that they know you more than you do. So you

Verses 2 & 3:

Verse lyrics (line 2): take it down, 'noth-er pill to swal-low.

2. Well, mis-ter bring____ me down, well, you, you like to bring____ me down, don-cha?
3. Mis-ter play____ your games, on-ly got your-self____ to blame when you

But I ain't lay-in' down, ba-by, I ain't go-in' down. Can't
want me back____ a-gain. But I ain't fall-in' back____ a-gain, 'cause I'm

no-bod-y tell me how it's gon-na be. No-bod-y gon-na make a fool out of me, ba-by.
liv-ing my truth with-out your lies. Let's be____ clear, ba-by, this is good-bye.

148

NOT OVER YOU

Words and Music by
GAVIN DeGRAW and RYAN TEDDER

Not Over You - 9 - 1

Chorus:

Not Over You - 9 - 3

152

Not Over You - 9 - 4

Verse 2:

154

ONE MOMENT IN TIME

Words and Music by
ALBERT HAMMOND and JOHN BETTIS

Medium ballad

Verse 1:

1. Each day I live, I want to be a day to give the best of

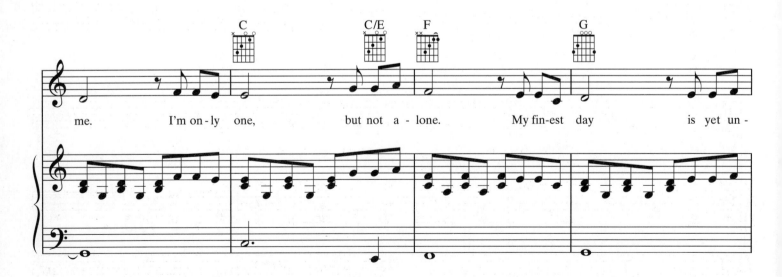

me. I'm on-ly one, but not a - lone. My fin-est day is yet un-

One Moment in Time - 5 - 1

Verses 2 & 3:

THE ONE THAT GOT AWAY

Words and Music by
KATY PERRY, LUKASZ GOTTWALD
and MAX MARTIN

Bright rock beat ♩ = 138

1. Sum-mer af-ter high school, when we first met,___ we'd make out in your Mus-tang to Ra-di-o-head.___ And on my eigh-teenth birth-day, we got match-ing tat-toos.___ Used to

The One That Got Away - 7 - 1

167

The One That Got Away - 7 - 5

PRICE TAG

Words and Music by
CLAUDE KELLY, BOBBY RAY SIMMONS,
LUKASZ GOTTWALD and JESSICA CORNISH

Moderately slow ♩ = 88

(with pedal)

Verse:

1. Seems like ev - 'ry - bod - y's got a price.___ I won - der how they sleep at
2. We need to take it back in time___ when mu - sic made us all u -

sim.

night, when the sale comes first and the truth comes sec - ond. Just stop for a min - ute and
nite, and it was - n't low blows and___ vid - e - o hoes. Am I the on - ly one get - ting

Price Tag - 6 - 1

Chorus:

Chorus:

SMOOTH CRIMINAL

Written and Composed by
MICHAEL JACKSON

178

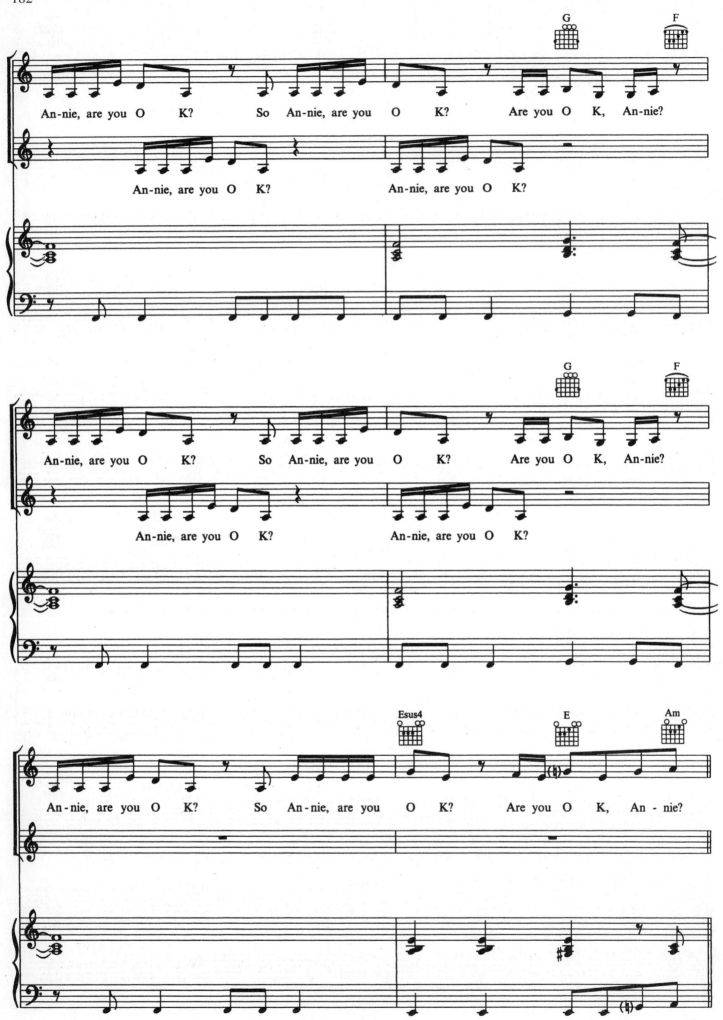

186

Smooth Criminal - 12 - 11

SOLDIER

Words and Music by
GAVIN DeGRAW

Verse 1 (sing 1st time only):

1. Where did all the peo-ple go? They got scared when the lights went low.

Verse 2 (sing 2nd time only):

2. Fun-ny, when times get hard, at the last mo-ment, when you're s'pposed to charge,

Soldier - 6 - 1

Chorus:

SOMEBODY THAT I USED TO KNOW

Words and Music by
LUIZ BONFA

Verse 3:

Girl:

3. Now and then I think of all the times you screwed me o - ver,

but had me be-liev-ing it was al-ways some-thing that I'd done.___

But I don't wan-na live that way, read-ing in-to ev-'ry word you say.

RED SOLO CUP

Words and Music by
**BRETT BEAVERS, JIM BEAVERS,
BRAD WARREN** and **BRETT WARREN**

202

you are the Ab - bott un - to my Cos - tel - lo. And you are the fruit of my loom.

Red so - lo cup, you're more than just plas - tic. You're more than a - maz - ing, you're

more than fan - tas - tic. And be - lieve me that I'm___ not the least___ bit sar - cas - tic when

I look at you___ and say:

Red solo cup, you're not just a cup.
You're my, you're my...friend. Yeah.
Thank you for being my friend.

rit.

a tempo

Chorus:

Red so - lo cup,   I fill you up;   let's have a par -

ty,   let's have a par - ty.   I love you

red so - lo cup.   I lift you up;   pro - ceed to par -

ty,   pro - ceed to par - ty.

Spoken:

Verse 2:
Now, I really love how you're easy to stack.
But I really hate how you're easy to crack,
'Cause when beer runs down in front of my pack,
Well, that, my friends is quite yucky.
But I have to admit that the ladies get smitten
Admirin' how sharply my first name is written
On you with a Sharpie when I get to hittin'
On them to help me get lucky.
(To Chorus:)

WE ARE YOUNG

Words and Music by
NATE RUESS, ANDREW DOST,
JACK ANTONOFF and JEFFREY BHASKER

Moderately ♩ = 120

Verse 1:

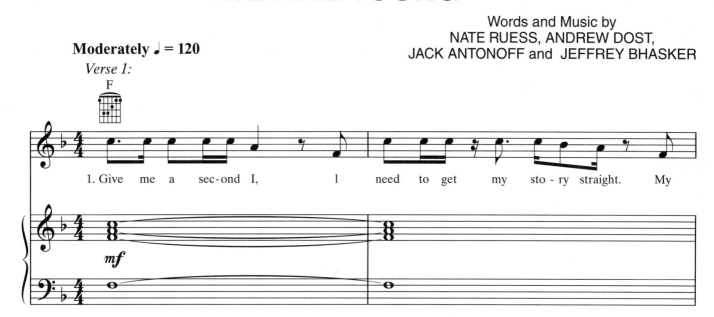

1. Give me a sec-ond I, I need to get my sto-ry straight. My

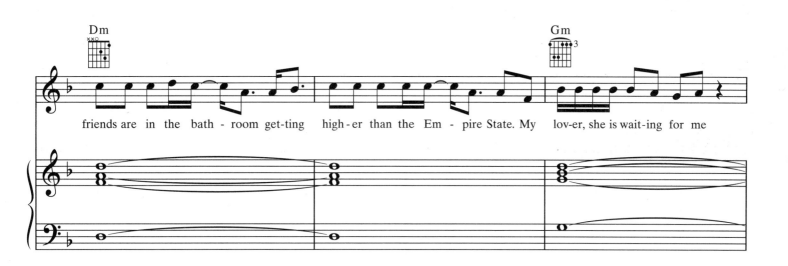

friends are in the bath-room get-ting high-er than the Em-pire State. My lov-er, she is wait-ing for me

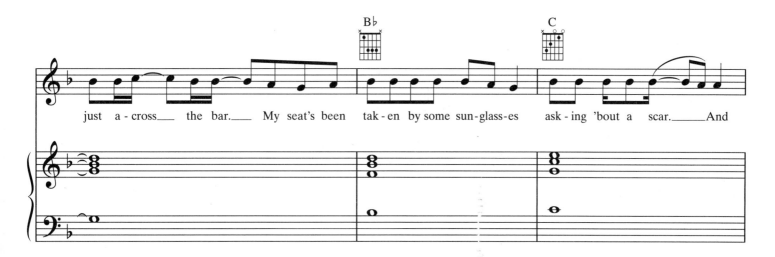

just a-cross___ the bar.___ My seat's been tak-en by some sun-glass-es ask-ing 'bout a scar.___ And

We Are Young - 7 - 1

Chorus:

210

We Are Young - 7 - 4

§ *Chorus:*

WHO SAYS

Words and Music by
PRISCILLA RENEA and EMANUEL KIRIAKOU

Verse 1 (sing 1st time only):

Verse 2 (sing 2nd time only):

Who Says - 6 - 1

216

Who Says - 6 - 3

WHEN WE STAND TOGETHER

Lyrics by
CHAD KROEGER

Music by
NICKELBACK

*Recorded in B♭m with Guitar capo 1.

When We Stand Together - 5 - 1

224